Once Out of Despair

Written By: Camari Nicole Sparks

I0456187

Once out of Despair

Camari Nicole Sparks ©2016

Table of Contents

- The alarm clock
- The hearse driver
- The queen of man
- Mom and Dad
- A reality
- My Best Friend
- The Journey
- The love affair
- In a late October month
- The highlight of my day
- After winter
- The devotion of business
- My monster
- Untitled 2
- My midnight romance
- The butterfly's sting
- Me and China
- If I fell in love with someone different
- The fairytale of fall
- The angel meeting
- That year
- The clown I fell in love with
- The spotlight lover
- If love ever got there
- When we fall in love

- On the evening bus
- The second Tuesday of the month
- On valentine's day
- Momma
- Me and You

About the Author

Camari Nicole Sparks born on Jan 7th 2003 with an interest in greater learning she embarks on the path of knowledge at a young age. That happens to be a very unique individual who enjoys helping others and even put herself last if it came down to it with dreams of visiting Paris and other great destinations. Furthermore being determined to become something great in society in the present time she is living. Knowing that to many doesn't even come close to having a chance. Nevertheless she doesn't look at her age as a factor not to do but entirely the opposite with the support of her loving friends and family. She does a marvelous job at keeping everything balanced.

Dedication

For the world for this is my heart, this is the heart I want you to see. I want you to hear .I want you to understand better for the people the world can live without. However the people who have dampened the trust but still are going for the stars. To my gone but never forgotten grandma Helen ,why did you let cancer get the better of you? Furthermore I can't leave out uncle B for you are the one who raised me but, why did you let cancer get the better of you also? Nevertheless my Aunt ,you left me to die in the state I was in and I prospered in spite of, My happiness ,you've gone away a macabre distance. God was like my best friend a while ago. Now my momma! The best momma there ever was in my opinion. The dad I never got to meet I feel sorry for you not because you're not in my life but because of the success I have achieved and continue to achieve without you but you could have had a great daughter all around that would have gave you something to brag about. Now since, you died, and the funeral was never arranged. To my main love, my heart because you have took the beating for me. The alcoholic that took me for granted, I wish you would of fell for someone else. I wish you would have stayed where you came from. My brain on the other hand never got a chance to understand you, but you are quite a brain, being a mystery and still managed to have earned my heart, but since we are one I prefer you to go but that's quite impossible to find something better. For my true love you were always there and you listened. For the world, for sometimes you are worth talking to.

Introduction

To the world for whoever may read "Once Out Of Despair" I was wondering if you see the sunshine, for there is no sunshine where I am. Where the graves lay, as I dig this hole, to bury my fleshly heart it is time to use the stony heart made of the best cement you could find. That a man once made for me but anyway I truly wrote this book to warn the world of the hell that is waiting when you make your last mistake, like I did. I've been washed away by the waves of the days and I hope that the world gets this, because time has been going by quickly these days a true sign of the end times that leaves my stomach churning like the makings of fresh butter, my days to long unforgettable daydreams, and my nights to nightmares.

Enduring so many breaking moments didn't really have a trusting ear or at least that what I thought. However I turned to the only option that was available and wouldn't disturb anyone my trusty pen and paper as a band aid to stop my bleeding heart, to numb the pain and last but not least warn the world.

The Addict's Advice

The world has always had a
sour taste as a salty blue ocean
as its tongue

As some too good demon

As its salty tongue and the
brain of a bad habit

Of people gone fraught

Amen to the long lost love

Whose love is now a sin

to sleep with the lover's wife
was now known as a sin

as the world begin to eat
boiled candies drink acid wine
and live to drink alcohol

in the dead day of it all I hope
he sees me there in the
opening of paradise where he
bled trying to be that lover of
mine

he built his heart of bricks and
wrote my name at the very top

and kissed me with his salty
tongue and since then my soul
was infected

Infected with a fuzz

a fuzz of bacteria and moss

for I knew better than to wait
for him to come around but
wasn't he the night in
diamonds when he gave me
the crown?

And carried me to the throne?

And handed me the scepter?

Then asked me to run away, to
a different kingdom?

And kissed me with his salty
tongue, and died that very day

For the world of sins and
paradise were too much for
him to take and they left his
body next to her the woman
he left for me and what a fool
he was to do that leave a
beauty for me

To the long last love

I don't know if this will ever
get to you for it has passed
through so many hands, but if
you ever get this I want you to
know, I'm sorry.......

I should have mentioned me
leaving that day you asked me
to marry you. In front of the
King of heaven, you know I
loved you still....

Even when you could not stop
drinking,

So tell me does your heart still
mourn over that moonlight
when we tried to picture the
stars?

 So tell me does your heart
still mourn over that winter
you took my heart away?

You know I wrote that book
for you the book about
summer

I told that woman to give it to
you because I still loved you.
If you are still well and the
beer didn't get the better of
you I want you to know I'm
sorry…….

But I'm going to try with all
my might to make it without
you.

Without the Witch's Humor

The callus of my heart in the
bottom is where I felt him

He asked to marry me and go
unto the paradise with him as
the paradise queen and make a
city of memories

To soak and spa in champagne
and it probably would of
happened if he didn't die that
way

Pimples on his fingernail
mercy in the vase

And I fell in love with a
romance that lies dead on his
face

Prince charming and the
massacre of beauty and the
beast and once the rats were
through with him

He left life to the glass the
glass of alcohol that stood in
his way

As he broke out in emeralds
his doll face died that way

after he promised me peace in
hell

The devil took him away......

Once in Paris

I know that all the while he
loves her.

 My heart just cripples up

My body cripples up and all
the while he does it he never
thinks to look up

And as his wife leaves him for
love, he cries within the night

He must not have known that I
am still here thinking about
him

The horrid in his eyes and
every night he thinks of her he
never thought to look in the
jar I am sitting in.

I made him a paper heart and
it is so pretty

I made it just for him but all
the while he loves her his
heart cripples up

And once a day I see him I see
his heart die out and one day it
died completely but never

once did he come and get the
heart I made for him.

So after a while I gave up
gave up on the paper heart it
held love and everything (as
the time kept fading away) I
crawled up out the jar, I saw
him sitting there and I walked
away from him his lover he no
longer loved

Midnight prayer

The last time I was happy was
before then

Before he drew the world in
the sky and the upper view of
the ocean he drowned within
the sky

He bled within the sky and his
blood shed in the lighting
storm with not a shred of rain

And his blood shed in the
ocean with not a shred of rain

And he smiled to the blinding
stripes alcohol took his life so
young so he never got a
gravestone except his very
home

He dug out a grave in HELL
to be put to rest and in Heaven
she dug her grave to put
herself to rest and it was
casually known as a suicide,
the homicide of it all but
better known as a good day
for a baby girl was born and

lived with the paradise the
paradise of it all

Until reality came and packed
within her mind the saint
called it misery the priest
declared it blind so over
underneath of the ocean is
where the love sits with polka
dots on its face. For every
time a marriage went without
it

The cat refused to marry me .

And so did that man before he
died he refused to marry me.

My shadow refused to marry
me, marry me under the stars
……..where the sky is bleak

For the man of the summer

The world did not know how
to look at it the diamond heart

It sat inside his chest with an
iron valve and blue blood
pumped through the dreadful
veins that were made of thin
red wine and filtered by a thin
white silk and it beat inside

the man's chest and the world
did not know how to look at it

The diamond heart it sat
inside his chest and not a
person could get in there

Into the diamond heart into
my lover's heart.

To compose or Not

The musician gave up on his
composing around this
dreadful time

The time I went without
knowing the long lost love
was mine

God had made him just for me
to patch up the enormous hole
in my heart

I never said hi to him…

I didn't get his name….

Because he was so beautiful
we went in separate ways he
went to find me

I went to find him

The man God made for me

And the musician gave upon
his composing around this
dreadful time

The time I went without
knowing the long lost love

was mine and he was so
beautiful

He did not deserve me I did
not deserve him

I wonder if he has turned
around and gave up on me

I would hate to disappoint him

The man God made for me to
give me a brand new heart

To hold me in his arms and
whisper in my ears romantic
proverbs and tell me I was
worth the trip sitting on the
ledge thinking of dying

And the musician gave up on
his composing around that
time that dreadful time

When I went without knowing
the long lost love was mine

To build a city of stars with

To live in the best part of time

And the musician gave up on
his composing around that
dreadful time

The time I went without
knowing that beautiful man
was mine

The accident

The summer of the accident
she made a gift for me

A salty nectar pie to eat with
the trees

The cream of nectar coming
out and I did not eat one piece

For such a death such a
cremation was no longer
special

To die within your lover's
reach was no longer special

Was no longer worth the time
to deal with the pressure

To convince the world to love
again

The people in the ditch who
wait for the cars to come to
watch them come by

And the people in the house
who watch the time go by

Without him without the long
last love who lived in an

alcoholic paradise and made a
woman a man and it wasn't
good luck

The painting never fell? Not
even in Hell's fire

The painting never fell……

Just at dawn

To my first best friend if you
ever were

Just an optimist, she thought
of beauty

The horrid asleep in the sky
and we dreaded what would
happen

If the mayor did not get there
in time

If the long last love did not get
there in time

The sadness all over the sky
and sadly he never got a
chance to see it

My heart bled out in the skies
just below the heavens not a
speck of happiness to be
found.

The funeral home music

The funeral home music
someday

Some of the time when I get
done digging this this hole

Success will fall through

True love will fall through

The days will fall through

The dead man will fall though

The heavens will fall through
because he never did

Because sunshine never did

Because the gravestone never
did

Because the casket never did

Let that man tell it he knew
my face from somewhere

He knew my heart from
somewhere

It was buried alive by the days
by the time

By the dead people

By that woman she said I was crazy and maybe I really am

That man said it himself one morning over tea one morning over alcohol one morning over a good day

I loved that boy so bad but he hasn't fell down here yet

I guess he's just a boy I used to love but he must still remember me

That last boy I loved......if he lives to read this I hope he can imagine the way I feel inside

The way I feel as I dig my heart out with this shovel you would not believe all the soil that is in here all the mud that is in here

 There was really no room for him…

Fake

The fake tears cried at the
funeral was the reason they
stayed sane

For the death of the world
died that very day

To keep your smile fraught
and keep your frowning joyful

At the wedding at the funeral
home

Where the morgue saw them
walking down the aisle to the
paper dream at my very
funeral

Where I died trying to be at a
place I built myself in the
daydream of my nightmare

Every day in the grave

That boy I loved I know he
loved me because that night
we sat under the stars and he
pointed to the darkest place up
there and he said we were
going to meet there one day

We'll sneak out of heaven for
the night and build a little city
out of stars and he kissed me.
And he held me

I remember it like it's
happening now. He held me
so tight and he kissed me
under the stars and he held me
over him and he pointed to the
darkest part of the sky and he
told me one night we were
going to build a city of stars
there and I looked at where he
was pointing

He died of a heart attack the
next day sometime in the
horrid morning but sometimes
looking at the stars I see
where the darkness was and
there is already a spec of light

there he has already started
building without me

The Medicine Effect

When the medicine entered
my system

In ways I can regret I saw him

He asked to walk with me
over to the painting shop

Deep within the trees and
there he left me

He took my soul and gave it to
the man next door I guess he
was in love after all

I guess my heart was meant
for the fall the fall of
raindrops on my skin in the
optimist of it all

Sometimes I sit trying to
remember his face he died
when he was put in his grave
but wasn't he my long lost
love?

When God took him away and
buried him on top the paradise

Where I could not visit

Where I could not see him

Buried on top of paradise

where he died trying to get

where he died trying to be

Sunday in the Grave

Some morning

Somehow

Somewhat

 Somewhere

A mimicking love in
someone's heart left one for
another

Another anonymous soul that
love fought in the past

In Hell in the ripped up bag

I hope you find your hope in
this trash can before he takes
out the bag

I hope you find your money
and gold in the trash can
before he takes out the bag

That woman married her soul
and like that it was brighter

But the best thing to do would
to be to let the sun shine and
you just be the writer

So why not now you don't
love what you see?

You must go a little bit deeper

So why not now you don't
love what you see?

You are getting a little bit
brighter…

After the rain

He was so beautiful until
raindrop came and slid down
his body in the lighting storm

The minute God was not
watching the raindrop took his
beauty

The minute the world was not
watching and once beauty left
the door was locked and
bolted and went unto the
misery for beauty was never
forgotten

When it jumped off the bridge
and the door was locked and
bolted it was day 105 of
therapy when the truth came
out and laid upon the day bed

Perfection was not yet the
word for there was a witness
an eye witness

Who saw it all when the
raindrop came and slid down
his body but stopped unto his
chest to see if the heart was
broken and when it was the
raindrop slid down unto the
ground

Until the very place he stood
was different and I saw it from
the diner's window it changed
him

And his body was in callus for
the beauty it had left and left
him in the flower stems'
master bedroom as he watched
beauty leave the maid brought
the extra towels the priest
brought up the bible

As he watched beauty leave
and I saw it from the diner's
window and it was since then
known as a tragedy

The dreadful operation the day
the surgeon came and the
medicine entered his system
the musician brought up the
violinist

The lover brought up the love

But all of this didn't matter for
the man's beauty was gone

I fell…

Once I fell in love I saw it

The opening of the flesh in my
lover's heart

It killed him that way all the
time he tried to change and
still remained the same

The same drunk he was before
he kissed me.

That way his heart torn up in
shreds and left the whole town
in horror in the city of the
shed

In the city of the world to
crown the newly wed

Untitled 1

The sun is as dry as the night

 The nigh made a nightmare
from scratch

All day I have let blood soak
through my brain now it's my
heart's turn

My heart has now went dry
my wings are to heavy
something in me has bled out.
But all the while that woman
and her air conditioner stay
tucked within her house there
was nothing to the cricket
except it was really blessed
and it owned a whole field just
for himself

My best friend my best friend
is she somewhere dead? Her
body it is soul less it sits in
some man's bed

If luck passes you by never
call it back because then it
will think you need it.

Luck is what killed the
buzzard he scratched his ticket
every night

Scratched that ticket until he
had no need for his life
whenever I cry he presses his
fingers into mine.

Whenever I cry the dead man
kisses my neck and leaves my
skin so dry

God bless the angel she is not
saved

God bless me as I jump this
cliff who knows what lies
below, never kiss a dead man
who knows who waits below
at romance

When the sky is dry.......

Mushroom Soup

The quality man, a man who
makes his money trying to
convince people he is making
it walked by me with a heavy
heart

His skin could not fit his face
could not fit his personality if
there were ever such a thing

If such a thing could ever be
he must of all saw the world
waiting on him, the guilt all in
his pants. For he knew what
he did

Sometime all day and he was
now divorced but not because
his woman knew but because
the guilt had left and that must
be what the sex love is guilt
all in your heart

Guilt all in your gut

Gilt all in your clothes that
little girl did not deserve
it...the fashion show, the
fashion show, the sweat

dripped in her coffee and the
memory did too

Dreams turn into nightmares
by morning

Turn to death by morning but
who am I to use death's name
in vain he deserves a lot more
respect and so did that
sunshine that dreadful day it
deserved a lot more respect. It
would be a shame not to make
the world yours while you
can. The death mare comes at
the dawn of morning and the
dreadful Christmas day when
some false god that goes by
the name of santa leaves until
morning

The last time

The last time I saw him he had
a love look on his face. He
had a dreadful dread, sitting
upon his face for he loved me
still and ran unto the dream
land with me, me ahead of
him and it was better known
as a romance, the dread of it
all or otherwise known as a
secret, for his wife said to
never know

Yet even in the spotlights the
wife said to never know

For she had a fantasy in her
head, one I was said to never
know and deep into paradise I
ran, the thorns runs up my
knees and he followed me and
looked unto the dreadful lock
that separated him and me

He promised me the world,
the world with diamonds and

gems and he loves me, he
loves me still

He kissed me on the lips and
ran unto the dream land with
me where I was left and never
once did I see him again
except for only once, and
when I saw him he looked at
me, the dread all in his eyes
all night, even in the night of
morning down underneath the
spotlight

Underneath the dread of
Heaven, underneath the Hell
and it was better known as a
romance, the dread of it all

The plastic heart the lover's
heart it died that very day and
went unto the paradise where
it was never

seen again, death strikes under
the spotlight with only dust to
be seen

And died under the spotlight
with only love to be seen….

If you could of seen it

My love died of a back pain
…must have been all the
cracks I stepped on

Must have been all the money
I stepped on

If that heart pumped oil it
would explain his love for
cars. If that soul was made of
money it would explain why
she was soul less

The rainbow wrapped around
her hair up within the stars
and never once did she look
down seeing the hurt in his
eyes

Never once did she look down
and see tears in my eyes

I guess that's how best friends
work that leave some kind of
tears in your eyes they leave
some star in your eyes

They leave stars in your eyes
and that is what I cry for, I
have too many stars in my
eyes and that is why the
woman hates my smile

I have too many stars in my
eyes and that is why God stays
beside me because I have a
fickle heart

But stars all in my eyes……

The alarm clock

When the alarm clock was
dismissed sitting on the
golden street of light I felt the
sadness

The sadness crept in his skin
and it lurked there for the rest
of his life and all he wanted
was a best friend to talk to

To go unto paradise with him
but he never got a friend so he
never went to paradise with
fear of going alone and they
said he died in the mansion

The mansion of stones and
bricks and of course the short
circuit, circuit of the day

The rats and roaches they
crawled within his skin so
amen to the happiness it
ceased the greatest sin

Amen to the blessing it ceased
the greatest sin

On top the golden street of
light in paradise where the
sadness was

Where the long lost love was
but would never be

The Hearse Driver

The woman who claimed the
body took her spouse to
France where her spouse was
buried beside her husband's
grave

When time to mourn she dug
the grave up and the woman
came crawled inside to sleep
but got not a spec of rest

The curtains crawled up the
legs of that man's summer
dream in which he slept all
day planning to marry me

The ring of emerald straw and
white silk diamonds and a
precious death in there with a
French vanilla setting sitting
on the rooftop of the earth but
still not by the heavens

Sitting by the God himself but
still not in the heavens

Marrying your valentine but
still not in the heavens

Thank God for the alcohol it
keeps that man alive

 Thank God for the devil's bad
luck it broke him out in hives
for telling that girl she was not
good enough

For talking in her dreams
making her give up her life
she meant something to me

Under the aloe plant he sits
waiting to be healed for what
he allowed in him now was
finally real and went to his
brain and stayed there

When the nightmare became
real

The queen of Man

Draw a portrait of the glass of
wine hoping to stop the
addiction of a love affair

For as the man slept around
his wife was to be killed by a
buzzard down the street who
had not eaten in days

The woman had no way of
knowing she was better dead
than to sit and wait for her
husband to come home which
he never did

The ocean breeze came
through the door the buzzard
creeped on in but to his
surprise the woman was gone
heading for the bridge

The threw her baby boy off
first then her wedding ring she
jumped herself but was quite
not dead the blood soaked
through her dress she saw her
husband

He looked at his wife he
introduced the woman to her it

was his sister the wife broke
out in tears for her marriage
was over

She died there crying on the
street the morgue came by and
got her

To the crematory she went
buried next to her baby her
husband died of a stroke that
morning

That morning it was his turn
to be carried away for he still
couldn't believe it his
soulmate thought of him that
way…

Mom and Dad

That man who wrote of
paradise must of saw it past
the leaves the leaves that
covered the grave he left

When he made his dreams a
reality for his woman who left
him to fend for himself

She wore the ring around her
neck so it would not get stuck
on her finger and be forced to
cut it off but looking at the
love affair you would not
guess it was from the heavens

The king of the world planned
it himself one morning talking
of our dreams to give love a
spark again

To drench in unfaithfulness to
spa in pills hoping that in the
end the world would Love
again

A reality

I have been in Hell and stayed for 32 weeks…36 weeks….91 weeks. I have been in this situation for 91 week but all the while that boy has been in my heart and there he sits in the left valve wrapped in my veins because I loved him because he tried to kiss me that day and I had to let him go because I could never take him to hell with me. Knowing I couldn't keep him safe so in my heart his memory sits his body in the stars and there it is next to my sanity

My sanity is all the way up in the stars and there it is next to my sanity

So is the little girl's soul it was hung to death by a star

So was my lover a long time ago his body was hung by a star

My guilt was hung by a star
and so is God's place for me it
was hung to death by a star

His memory His memory it
stays within my heart and
there the devil can't find him.
He is buried within my heart.

My Best Friend

I know I loved him and he
loved me

But I had to go because if not
I couldn't save myself

From all our rights and
wrongs

But he was my biggest fan

He ran with me until I told
him to stop

So I could get settled here for
now in life

Where the glitter doesn't glow
and I watched him walked
back, I could tell he didn't
want to go and he wanted to
stay with me but I told him to
go back home

I wanted him to stay as well
but I was falling apart I was
busy with everything

But he was my biggest fan, he
loved me

And as I built my life up
instead of building up his he

went on the other side and
helped me with mine and he
never left my side until I
asked him to

But he didn't want to leave
but I made him go

But I love him still

I wanted him to have a chance
at happiness

I wanted him to make his life
better but he wanted a life
with me

But I told him to leave
because I didn't believe him

The Journey

That day she kissed him
started the week. He took her
by the hand and showed her a
fairytale scene but it was over
in a matter of seconds as if it
was all a dream and instead of
holding hands he cried to
himself in the lonely night
begging her to stay

But due to greed and
nervousness the angels took
her away and she was left
alone on someone else death
bed

And he was left alone on
someone else death bed

Remembering the moments
with tears streaming down his
cheeks but neither sad nor of
happiness just somewhere in
between and he sat alone
thinking about his love of life

That could not be his past.
The summer night a night was
there that night he kissed her
and he showed her a fairytale

scene but it was over in a matter of seconds as if it was all a dream

And it was over in a matter of seconds as if it were all a dream as if it all were planned in a dream

A royal blue sunrise was there and a pink diamond ring was there and he fell in love with her. She gave him her hand and they ran to the fairytale moment it took years to make but it was over in a matter of seconds and then she was gone

Then the love of his life was gone

Gone to somewhere far and near and a mile next to last and she left him for happiness she saw the sunrise blue but left anyway

And let his hand go that night all because he forgot to say "I Love You"

The Love Affair

If the love was real

The marriage wasn't
necessary

The happiness wasn't
necessary

The life wasn't necessary

If the love was real

Then I guess I would take but
I couldn't get it

I'm afraid the world would
take it so I took him anyway

My favorite man who did not
leave my side

Who did not leave my heart
because he loved me more
than he have ever loved
anyone

In a late October Month

A thick satin curtain was torn
down for the woman wanted
to see night but once the
curtain was down she could
only see the night it was a
blue darkness that lay dead in
the eyes of a once beautiful
woman until the skies had
died and left the earth
merciless

That day the blue skies died
and left the earth in a
depression a depression so
thick that when a day came
along not an hour was missed

Missed to the dread of a once
beautiful curtain that was torn
down in a disgraceful attempt
to knock the world down and
see the sunshine again.

See the happiness again that
was lost a life time ago due to
death and sins and the awful
day a love was lost due to
greed and dread

When the girl came up
missing in the ocean cause she
ventured off the sea in a
desperate attempt to save him
and her from the dread of a
romance that was to take place

I wonder could I ever be
happy again now that I've
gotten sick inside due to death
and sins

The woman tore down the
thick satin curtain hoping to
see the sunshine again

Hoping to see the happiness
again but over here in the
sorrow it no longer does exist

Due to one bad romance it no
longer existed

When the heart is compressed,
compressed until it cannot
escape what mind torments it
with

When the man forgot of me
but in no way was missed over
here in the sorrow

It no longer exist due to a one
bad fairytale

It no longer exist for the ones
who want to see it again

The highlight of the day

One day waking up from a
winter nightmare I saw him

The one who kissed me on top
of a brilliant star and ran on
the skies with me

Now I have debated how to
tell the story of romance but
only dread was dreamed as we
crawled into the marge and
never seen again for the rest of
the summer of the love affair
that loved the world and took
time for the talking had we
ever dreamed of love

We dreamed that way in a pit
less hell where the bravest
couldn't take

 I wonder is he still alive the
knight in shining armor

Up on top of the brilliant start
to peer within the heavens and
overcome the dreadful news
that an angel is but pure less

and if we dreamed of love we
dreamed it that way climbing
the only staircase to heaven of
the lucky heart where some
die trying to be when the love
story start to falls apart and
makes a masterpiece that is
when old gets disgraceful

That is when old gets battered
and shameful due to life and
love

When neither one is
happening to the people who
want to see what's willing to
be seen in true loves horrid
morning

The time of marriage and love
making of every single wrong
that took place that day.

After winter

Over underneath a spotlight
that had blinded countless
eyes I saw him

The man I had waited to see
he made me come alive again

Over underneath a moonlight
that made the night not as dry
I saw him that man I had
waited to see made me happy
again

Simply because I had waited a
long time for him to hold me
that way and spin me around
the world and yell in the
empty castles falling more in
love by the days

He lifted me to the stars; he
lifted me up past the rain, until
I could see the world, until I
could see happiness

Over underneath a daytime
that had pumped back into life
I saw him that man I had

waited to see he made me
myself again

He made me consider love
again

He made me consider
romance

The devotion of Business

I fell in love only once and it
was to a man

Who left me for the feel of
romance and kisses on his
skin and left me one dry
morning

My heart he ate up years ago
and there he died of food
poisoning

That many years ago I fell in
love only once

And it was with a man who
left me for business that lasted
until he ate up my heart

Many years ago in the dry
morning of romance kisses on
his skin and due to that
fairytale moment I still, I still
love that man who gave me a
chance.

My Monster

I know that the monster under
my bed gets lonely sometimes
under there all by himself. So
I put my teddy bear down
there with him so his heart can
heal.

I know the monster under my
bed gets tired of living

So I crawl up under there with
him some nights and we talk
for hours

I know that monster under my
bed gets afraid sometimes all
by himself

So I always put a flashlight
under there for him, so he can
see some light

I know the monster under my
bed loves me

I taught him how to read and
write all the while no one else
loved us in the middle of the
night.

Untitled 2

When the accident occurred it
made faces turn blue and it
made a tornado of diamonds
and people left in the world
and it left the world dizzy
giving her a heart attack as she
jumped on the mountains and
claimed to see heaven from
there

As the accident occurred when
out of the glimpse of nowhere
she left the world last, last
from a happiness that rotted
somewhere in the past, when
mother nature sold her soul
and the people brought out the
cash to buy her place

When the accident happened
and left her a bitter rash on his
and my heart that day the
world gave up on us.

My Midnight Romance

Sometimes when I am awake
but still in bed in the dusk
before night that demon in my
head tells me stories of his
life, he use to have before the
evil took over, before the
dread took over and gave his
soul to the devil and left his
mind empty handed. He tells
me of the romances he wanted
to tell the world

He tells me fairytales and
running through the halls of
the cathedrals and fuzzy
winter gloves he tells me of
his beautiful dreams about a
love of his. Who he was to
marry in the summer. When
he got settled in my brain he
tells me of a Saturday where
he thought he would die alone
but when he saw my beautiful
home he knew he had a home
and this is the part that makes
me cry because I want to
make him happy but he

weighs on my brain and he
puts a dense fear on my heart.

 He tells me how he no longer
wants to be bad now he wants
to love and he twist and tosses
in my brain but I cannot tell
him to leave. I have become
one with him even though I
know he's killing me he is
taking my brain as his own but
that is his home right? I raised
him up whole but he is
making me decay but some
nights he tells me stories of
how his life used to be.

 He tells me of a dense
romance he teaches me to how
to climb the trees and to see
the above the skies he tells me
of a time he believed he would
die.

Then he goes to say that I
saved his life. He tells me
stories of the sunlight. The
ones I never got to see
because I am stuck being
depressed as we make our
masterpiece and he and I
make a brand new paint for

the world and dance in the
darkest halls as we fall in love
with each other. Climbing up
the walls as he tells me stories
of how he once was before
God dammed him a demon
due to the death of his brain
that caused him to kill my
heart.

The butterfly's Sting

Once a day a day before now
a day still in waiting for the
world

A day before

A day before I was most
miserable before the forlorn
days came

Before the doctors came and
took my blood away

Before the rings came around
my eyes

Before my lover carried on a
fairytale and ceased to watch
it die.

On the mountain of sustained
life, stained by candlelight
when nothing was no longer
worth it, worth the wounding
fights

Before I had to say goodbye to
my best friend, to my love, to
my beautiful life to cease into

moonlight whether it is neither
day nor night writing for the
man I love who could not get
into heaven

Writing for the muted girl
who could not explain the
reason that man with the suit
and tie does he love me still?
Or has business got the best of
him

That man I should of never
loved that last summer I ever
saw him venturing to
happiness and purpose at the
very same time has left a bitter
somber look to stain my very
eyes

I wonder if he sees me still?
That man I wanted to love but
never could for I was not
enough even when I gave him
my soul I still was not enough

I wish he would write

I wish he would call

But what am I ever to say? He
was a man I used to love

I wish I could convince him I
need him to come back home
because I love……..I love him
still, my best friend before I
was brought into love and
never seen again

Before I was brought into hell
and never seen again

Praying God would make me
beautiful again hoping the
king of heaven would see I
was worth his attention.

Me and China

Yesterday when the sky went
black and the stars and moon
paid the earth a little more
attention and the grass was
damp with rain and the ant
piles were damp with soil and
the little man's heart got
lighter.

Me and little china ran around
the yard air souls somewhere
in the stars and yes we were a
little bit out of our heads as
we ran and jumped on top of
the moon and the sun should
have seen us, we were up so
high, so high up. I felt my
heart start to cry

Me and little china were lost
in the wind, our souls they
jumped from star to star, they
jumped from star to star so
quick it made my heart start to
beat

In the midst of the darkness
my heart started to beat oh and
my feet they ran this way and
that oh and little china's feet
ran this way and that and the

darkness couldn't keep up.
We fooled then into thinking
that we would not be alright

Our hands were in the air. We
then look up and see a
rainbow in the sky

We saw the sunlight come.
We woke the sun up and we
both know we had power

The two best friends in the
world

If I fell in love with someone different

A massive heart built for me

Sadly I could not fit it in my chest, so pieces were slaughtered away. Piece by piece until I had the small one that I have today

Due to the pinkest diamond that made room for itself in my very eyes a pit way to the darkest Hell lays in my eyes I wonder if that was the reason after all

Why the story falls apart when I write of the massive heart built for me that held the things I love but that could not fit in my chest

So was buried alone

piece by piece was axed away until I have the rotting chunk that I possess today to fall in

love one way or another when
I see him again

that man that could never love
me you could tell by his smile
when his teeth rotted through
once he bit in the apple of a
dream meant for us two

A massive heart built for me
by the king of heaven but that
could not fit in my chest

So by piece by piece it was
taken. Taken to the grave that
sits alone

A massive heart built just for
me bigger than the earth

Bigger than the one I have
now that was taken piece by
piece by the king of Heaven
himself

For the heart was built for
someone else who could love
better than me for why would
he give a heart to the introvert

Who will love like me....

The fairytale of Fall

Before now when I was still
prospering in good health I
know for a fact that he would
always listen but I be damned
if he ever did. He just built my
heart up and showed me over
the peak he just gave me his
hand and we went running on
the dirt roads together. When
it was just him and me he just
kissed me under the star
lights, and spotlights on stage
but told me not a damn thing
of this horrid cage that he
locked me in

He just showed me in the
mirror what a beauty I was he
just made me fly all day and
night only to let me suffer he
just put his hands on my waist
as we both went around
bragging to the sunsets about
what we could make

Bragging to the sunsets about
a brand new day

Bragging to the sunsets that
we had come some way and
bragging g we did it together.
Me and the prince in waiting
me and my romance man who
out of the deed of everything
promised me his hand but he
never listened I just wanted
him to listen and he wouldn't
listen and that mattered most
of all

The Angel Meeting

The supporter of tense life
over ruled the nights

I was with him that man who
wanted me so and promised
me that mid-day I would fall
in love but that is when the
curse came

He tried to preserve me

He tried to marry me

But he was not that brave to
save me from the hell that is
built in my brain and he was
not brave enough to save me

And the story was told on a
stormy night when I fell for
him over in the London Rush

Where we have kissed
fighting over in the mountain
lake

Where we have kissed
fighting over in the hills of
Hell

Where we have kissed
fighting so that people could
live and love

That Year

Every day that year I thought
about it considering love again

Considering him again that
boy who offered me a chance
to be in the middle of his heart

Its empty in there, the blood
just comes and goes, I wonder
why there's nothing in here
just cobwebs and cracks I
cleaned up where I could but
it was not enough for the
moment I crawled out he died
and then there was dust.

But didn't he know I still
loved him? I wish I could of
seen his eyes he must have
been in pain. For once he built
out a cardboard horizion , he
was never seen again

But didn't he know I still
loved him? I wish I could
have seen his eyes, he must
have been in pain for once he
built a cardboard heart for me
and he was never seen again

but I still love him I know he
was in pain

For when his other honey left
with the kids he was never
seen again but I still love him

We were just the same our
hearts were molded together

The blood comes and goes we
could have been married on
top of the mountains so the
King of Heaven could see, but
I know he was still in pain, he
tried to tell me but I still love
him

I made him a place in the
middle of my heart where he
could of always been but once
he went to find happiness he
was never seen again

The clown I fell in love with

That man who talked bad of
me could never know how bad
I wanted him to hold me
around my waist and kiss me
every moment that gave us
breath to take and make me
smile for once even if it was
just for one day and take me
past the stars and take me so
far away that only moments
could take us back and could
only take our breaths away
how bad I wanted him to love
me, love until forever at least
but he thought I would hurt
him

But I never would he was the
beauty of my life

I wanted him by me every
night

I wanted him to look in my
eyes for once

I knew he was in pain for
every time he looked at me he
quickly turned away and he
never let me see his face

That man who I wanted so bad

I wanted to tell him I would
be good to him but he beat me
up with his words he built my
depression up but I love him
and I want him even though it
hurts and when I moved on I
got hurt again and he once
gone died.

The Spotlight Lover

Drowning in the sand of the
ocean waiting for the right
time to burst into Hell's front
door and demand redemption

The thread man…

The lucky man….

He married her that way and
ate with plastic spoons when
the world sung that day

Sung about the beauty that lay
dead in his eyes a skyscraper
tall statue of the lovers heart
but no room for the people

Only that one fair skinned girl,
who he made his bride who he
made his queen. I saw it for
myself what happened in the
room the room of paper
diamonds, love in brilliant
blue and pearl like settings

As he drowned in the sand of
the ocean waiting for the right
time to bust inside the heaven

doors and see above the skies
and he would of made it out of
bed to do this if he was ever
on time that man I loved more
than life who did not love me
at all

That man I loved more than
writing who did not love me at
all......

If love ever got there

It was a good three years ago
when I last saw that boy

The one who loved me more
than life who last saw me
whole

That boy with blue eyes

That boy with the pink heart

That boy with passion to make
me his love again

It was a good three years ago
when I last saw that boy the
one who loved me more than
life who last saw me whole
before I split up in pieces
before I got cracks in my skin
before I walked into that
grown man who made me
somber again

Who made me a perfect heart
wrapped in royal blue sins to
go with his royal blue suit he
wore at the cremation of a
once beautiful woman

A good three years ago when I
last saw that boy who made
me consider love again love
with a perfect thread heart to
feel what is worth feeling in
the nightmares meant to take
the carriage to paradise

Three good years ago when I
saw that boy last who was the
last one ever to see me whole

When we fall in love

When the surgeon declared
her blind, which mostly rained
all that day

When the world crawled out
her eyes and left the sunlight
pink and the days a dire past

When we left years in front of
us and were free at last

When we let the street lights
guide us

When we past the stars and
were left a dire restraint

When the dire days had died
but stayed wide awake to
watch us as we laughed in
happiness so real

It took a lifetime to make me
and that man who had the
brown eyes and the beautiful
smile

That brilliant man I wanted to
love me before the days had

died, before the dire days
came and took us back, and
the happiness we made for
ourselves- stabbed us in the
back when we fell in love

On the evening bus

That woman who made her
life of gems sewed her heart
with straw, so that when that
man came back he'd go in the
other direction. For once the
woman made her life of gems
reality had awaken and threw
glitter on her skin, and made
her heart back row and so she
covered it for herself when the
world became a sustained
wrong, when her honey went
to paradise to reunite with is
love in waiting, and left her
heart alone but left her with
the promise that he would
come back home, which was
more than my man gave me
the summer after last, when
everything we talked filled the
bitter past of every morning

The second Tuesday of the Month

The loveliest life anyone
could live is one where they
only have to suffer for a little
while

I have seen this life one time

When life was full of tiring
situations when happy
circumstances turned to
excruciating pains, it came
about it came up in a poem
that a beautiful life was a
brand new one but he was
beautiful wasn't he?

As he made his way in
cobwebs and dust

The loveliest life anyone
could live is one where they
only have to be tired for a
little while

I have seen this life one time it
used to be my own

Until I tied my heart to that beautiful idea and after that I haven't tied my heart with anything, anything ever again for there was nightmares took form the moment I made her my friend, the day I became a damned shame in the eyes of the tree that left a branch to protect my heart from the falling me

My lovely life

My beautiful life that day the dull dim lightbulb shone up in the sky then later was known as the sun, in the middle of the night before the nightmare came and left us confused for wasn't that man beautiful in the happiness of his dread that day the graves were dug, and they saw the body of the girl who once was me before I got tired and only had to suffer for a little while.

On Valentine's Day

He kissed her hand that night
and promised her the world

He gave her the ocean

He gave her the sun and no
one had anything to say. He
listened to her cry, to the
littlest cry

He still mourns over her tears
he talked her

When she felt alone and alone
she never had to be and afraid
she never was he stood her in
front of the world

And promised her she was
better and she blushed every
time she was with him and she
smiled every time she was
with him and she was happy
every time she was with him
because he loved her more
than life more than the world,
more than the things that take
breaths away in the romance

of the night he built her like a queen and made a massive heart and put her inside

Where she would not be hurt, where she would be safe, he was always there telling her about what they would do and saying they would do it together he had the eyes of a child he built his fairytale for her, his love of life, he would not let her cry. Except of tears of joy as he gave her the best life that you ever could see he sung to her the song a bird sung

A romantic hymn and when it was midnight it was just her and him. as he bowed to her in merry, not to leave his side and to keep they carriage waiting as they ran all day and night

To happiness

To romance

And gleam and sunlight and mystery hoping and praying they would never have to

leave and they lived there
forever, had love and romance

As they did not pursue
happiness but ran deep into it
and was caught there on
valentine's day as expected
and was caught there together
as expected

Momma

I have never known that love
that is brilliant blue but we
didn't know it together. We
never got a chance to go in
paradise, for when we got
there the door was locked so
we went empty handed, empty
minded and we talked of
sunshine and love when
neither one had a chance of
happening

Momma my best friend, the
best momma there ever was I
want you to know I love you,
let's just go unto a happiness
we never got a chance to have

Momma my best friend lets
make a brilliant blue light so
we can brag we did it together

Momma my best friend for
now those years was lost for
us let's make them over again
and get the thirty-seven years
back and make a brand new
way. We could stay in

happiness forever me and you
and we can get back the years
we lost me and momma my
best friend the best momma
there ever was happy birthday

Mirrored to the sun you are
better

Mirrored to the world you are
better there really is no thing,
no person that is better than
you

You brought my heart here

Now I am a the princess in
waiting and you put the crown
on my head, the moment God
started watching and made me
beautiful again

You restored me to myself
again

You are my hero

You got to be a queen

Even though you yell
sometimes and get pretty mad.
So I told that depressed voice
in my head to shut up while I
tell you I love you

Me and You

You were the sunshine of my
day

You had to be that brilliant
star shine up to make my day
because you were my love in
waiting

We flourished together in
dreams and when awaken

I could not help but to think of
you the way you looked at me

You still have my secret
locked in your heart it was a
story at first you know but
then it was real and I love you
even today

You and I made it real and we
made it worth it, we fell in the
pit of happiness watching the
stars look for us but we were
yet to be found. You showed
the sunlight still shone in my
eyes, you showed me how to
sneak on top of the moon

without the stars seeing us, you never left my side, and you were always there. We both had a fire that burned the sadness away. As long as you lived you did not leave my side because you wanted me so bad. When the sunlight still shone in my eyes you tied a bow around my heart and kissed me on the mountain peak so God himself could see. You and I were young and we had no clue what we were doing but we both wanted to be with each other forever but due to the cancer of life you are just the past and I loved you every day, I knew you but I never got a chance to tell you this cause I was afraid of rejection

To purchase additional copies please call

770-609-7384, 478-721-5389

Or email

cprompub@gmail.com

Also for comments, book signing events, and suggestions.